Contents

Any words appearing in bold, **like this**, are explained in the Glossary.

Germany

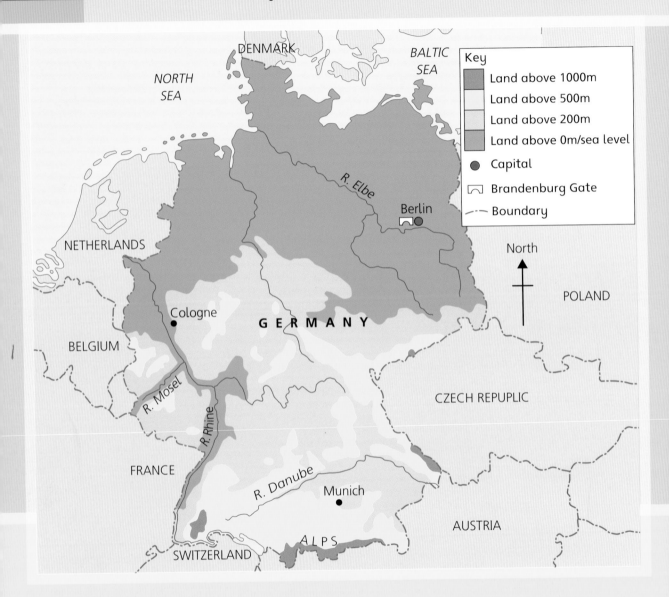

Key	
	Land above 1000m
	Land above 500m
	Land above 200m
	Land above 0m/sea level
●	Capital
⌒	Brandenburg Gate
-·-	Boundary

DENMARK

NORTH SEA

BALTIC SEA

R. Elbe

Berlin

NETHERLANDS

North

POLAND

Cologne

GERMANY

BELGIUM

CZECH REPUBLIC

R. Mosel

R. Rhine

FRANCE

R. Danube

Munich

AUSTRIA

ALPS

SWITZERLAND

Germany is a big country. It is in the middle of Europe.

There are many big cities in Germany, like Berlin and Cologne (below). Most people in Germany live in cities.

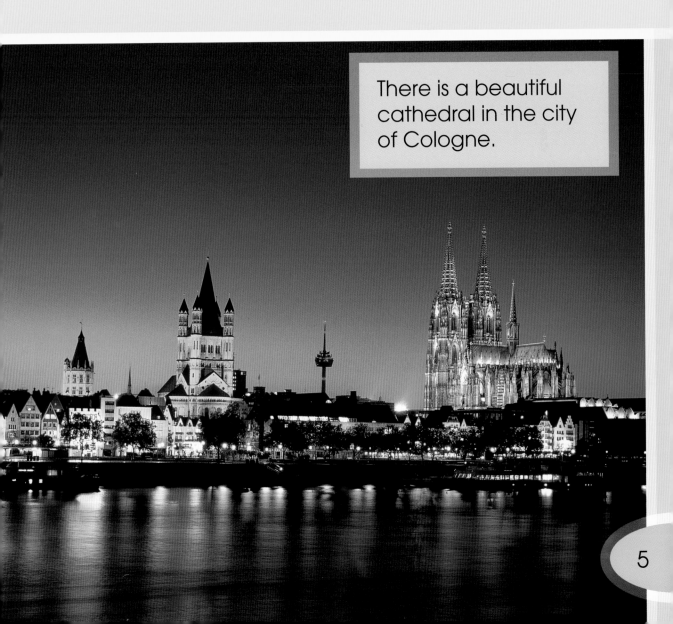

There is a beautiful cathedral in the city of Cologne.

Land

In the north of Germany the land is flat and low. There are **marshes**, and islands in the sea. Here the weather is wet and mild.

In the south of Germany are forests, **meadows** and mountains. The mountains are called the Alps. Winters here are very cold with lots of snow.

Summers in the Alps can be warm and sunny but there is still snow on the mountain tops.

Landmarks

Germany's biggest river is the Rhine. It is 1,320 kilometres long. Along the river banks are **vineyards**, and beautiful castles.

The Brandenburg
Gate is 200 years old.

This is the Brandenburg Gate. It stands in
the middle of Berlin. Berlin is Germany's
capital city.

Homes

Germany's towns and cities are crowded and busy. There is not much space for big houses and gardens. Many people live in flats.

In the countryside there are old farm houses. They have wide **sloping** roofs so the snow will slide off.

Farm houses in the countryside are often built from wood.

11

Food

In Germany, lunch is an important meal. There might be **schnitzel** with vegetables and mashed potatoes.

Sausage called wurst is a special German food. There are lots of different kinds of wurst. Some are eaten hot, and some are eaten cold, some are sliced, some are **spicy**.

Clothes

Germans wear **modern** clothes, like jeans and T-shirts. In cold winters people have to wrap up warm in thick coats and boots.

Clothing for festivals often have beautiful decorations.

At parties and festivals many Germans wear special clothes. They might wear leather shorts called lederhosen, and a cap with feathers like this boy.

Work

Many Germans have jobs in factories, offices and shops. They make cars, lorries, machines and **electrical goods**.

Farmers use big machines like these to cut wheat.

In the country, farmers keep cows and pigs. They also grow grain, potatoes and fruit. The weather and soil are good for farming.

Transport

There are many big **motorways** in Germany. There are train stations in every city, and busy airports.

Big ships carry coal,
steel and oil along
the rivers and canals.

On Germany's rivers and **canals** there
are ships and **barges**. On the River Rhine
ships from the sea can travel right into
Germany.

Languages

In Germany people speak German. Some German and English words sound nearly the same, like 'buch' and 'book', and 'haus' and 'house'.

In German there are two ways of speaking. One way you must use with adults and important people. The other way is for friends.

School

School starts early in Germany, at 7.30am. There is school on a Saturday too. But lessons always finish at lunchtime, and everyone has the afternoon off.

These children are going on a school trip to the zoo.

When they are in class German children study many subjects, including maths and German. They also have English lessons.

Free time

Many Germans like going on holidays. In the summer, families often go to the beach. In winter when it snows, some people go skiing in the Alps.

Many Germans love sport. They join sports clubs, and play tennis and football. They go walking and camping in the forests and mountains.

Germans enjoy cycling too.

Celebrations

Christmas is the most important celebration in Germany. There are special markets and funfairs. The streets sparkle with lights.

Every year in July there is a children's festival. Children dress up in costumes and parade through the streets.

The Arts

Germany is famous for its beautiful music. Beethoven and Schumann were German. They wrote music for **orchestras**, and for the piano.

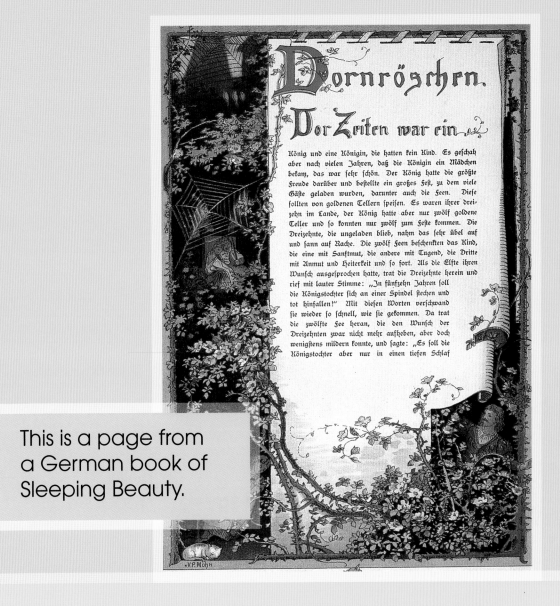

Dornröschen.

Vor Zeiten war ein

König und eine Königin, die hatten kein Kind. Es geschah aber nach vielen Jahren, daß die Königin ein Mädchen bekam, das war sehr schön. Der König hatte die größte Freude darüber und bestellte ein großes Fest, zu dem viele Gäste geladen wurden, darunter auch die Feen. Diese sollten von goldenen Tellern speisen. Es waren ihrer dreizehn im Lande, der König hatte aber nur zwölf goldene Teller und so konnten nur zwölf zum Feste kommen. Die Dreizehnte, die ungeladen blieb, nahm das sehr übel auf und sann auf Rache. Die zwölf Feen beschenkten das Kind, die eine mit Sanftmut, die andere mit Tugend, die Dritte mit Anmut und Heiterkeit und so fort. Als die Elfte ihren Wunsch ausgesprochen hatte, trat die Dreizehnte herein und rief mit lauter Stimme: „In fünfzehn Jahren soll die Königstochter sich an einer Spindel stechen und tot hinfallen!" Mit diesen Worten verschwand sie wieder so schnell, wie sie gekommen. Da trat die zwölfte Fee heran, die den Wunsch der Dreizehnten zwar nicht mehr aufheben, aber doch wenigstens mildern konnte, und sagte: „Es soll die Königstochter aber nur in einen tiefen Schlaf

V.P.Mohn.

This is a page from a German book of Sleeping Beauty.

Have you heard the story of Sleeping Beauty? This is a very old German **fairy tale**, written down by two brothers called Grimm.

Factfile

Name	The Federal Republic of Germany
Capital	Germany's **capital** city is called Berlin.
Language	German
Population	There are 82 million people living in Germany.
Money	German money is called the euro.
Religions	Most Germans are Christians but there are many other religions too.
Products	Germany makes chemicals, cars and lorries, machines and **electrical goods**.

Words you can learn

guten Tag (goo-ten targ)	hello
Auf Wiedersehen (owf vee-d-say-n)	goodbye
ja (ya)	yes
nein (nine)	no
danke schön (danke shern)	thank you
bitte (bitter)	please
eins (eye-ns)	one
zwei (svi)	two
drei (dry)	three

Glossary

barge a boat with a flat bottom. It can float in shallow water.

canal a river dug by people

capital the city where the government is based

electrical goods things like televisions and video recorders which use electricity

fairy tale a story where anything can happen

marshes flat, wet places

meadow grassy land

modern new, up-to-date

motorway a big, fast road. Often they have three lanes of cars going each way.

orchestra a group of people who play music

schnitzel fried meat in breadcrumbs

sloping leaning

spicy food with a strong, hot taste

vineyard place where grapes are grown

Index